A Teacher's Guide to Guided Reading

Contents

What Is Guided Reading?
The Importance of Leveled Books 2
Guided Reading Formats 2

The Guided Reading Lesson
Before Reading 3
During Reading 3
After Reading 3
Teacher Tips and Think-Alouds.............................4

Setting Up Your Classroom
Getting Your Students Ready for Guided Reading 4
Preparing Your Classroom 4
Your Guided Reading Schedule 5
Setting Up Literacy Centers in Your Classroom 5

Managing Your Classroom: A Practical Example
Class Profile 5
Guided Reading Groups 5
Schedule 5
What Are the Rest of Your Students Doing? 6

Placing Your Students in Appropriate Groups
Assessment of Reading Behavior 7
Administering an Assessment of Reading Behavior 7
  Selecting the Text 7
  Reading and Recording 8
  Checking Comprehension and Skills....................10
  Scoring the Reading 11
  Analyzing the Results 12
Other Assessments 13

Choosing the Right Books 14

Using Nonfiction Books for Guided Reading
The Guided Reading Process with Nonfiction Books 14
  Before Reading...15
  During Reading..15
  After Reading..15
Graphic Organizers 15

Appendix 1
Leveling Criteria 16

Appendix 2
Guided Reading Formats 22

Appendix 3
Strategy Prompts..25

Appendix 4
Sample Guided Reading Planning Form 27

Appendix 5
Blank Planning Form 28

Appendix 6
Assessment of Reading Behavior Teacher Score Sheet 29

Appendix 7
Error and Accuracy Rates 31

Bibliography 32

What Is Guided Reading?

Guided reading is an instructional reading approach that allows you to support a small group of approximately two to five students in learning, applying, and practicing effective reading strategies while they read from an appropriately leveled book. Guided reading provides the following benefits for both you and your students.

- It helps build a bridge between whole group shared reading and independent reading.
- It allows you to match students with texts that offer appropriate challenges yet ensure successful reading.
- It allows you to guide individual students in the reading process.
- It ensures that you are meeting the individual reading and skill needs of each of your students.
- It allows you to extend previous instruction and to introduce and model new skills and strategies.
- It provides you time to more effectively monitor individual students' strengths and needs.
- It allows students to work together and learn from each other.
- It allows students to become problem solvers and gives them the opportunity to explore and test their understanding of the reading process.

What's the Evidence?

The guided reading process is supported by the discussions of Tompkins, 1997; Fountas and Pinnell, 1996; Routman, 1991; Tancock, 1994; and Adams, 1990.

The Importance of Leveled Books

Reading development is characterized by four stages: early emergent, upper emergent, early fluency, and fluency. The Wright Group has twenty levels of books from Levels A through T, specifically designed to help students learn and practice the skills appropriate to each stage of reading development. At the earliest levels the books have simple language structures, repetitive sentence or phrase patterns, few lines of text on a page, strong illustration support, and easier vocabulary. As the levels progress, the books have less repetition, contain more lines of text on a page, and use longer sentences, more contextual support, and more advanced vocabulary.

Books at the early emergent and upper emergent stages can be easily correlated to Reading Recovery Levels 1 through 20. Levels A through T can also be correlated to many other guided reading leveling systems. Gradually leveled books will be the most successful means of meeting an individual student's needs in reading. (**See appendix 1 on page 16 for a more detailed look at the Wright Group leveling criteria and student outcomes.**)

It is important to use carefully leveled books at the students' instructional level for guided reading. Providing support at each student's instructional level is referred to as working within the "zone of proximal development" by Vygotsky (1962). This scaffolding helps transition students between what they know and what they still need to know. As students become confident at one level, they move to the next level of proximal development. In the beginning, students will need much more support in all areas of reading development. As they become more proficient in using reading skills and strategies, this support or scaffolding slowly decreases.

Guided Reading Formats

The Wright Group has developed six guided reading lesson formats to support readers at each stage of development. Each format of the guided reading process has a specific area of focus that provides the necessary scaffolding to ensure students' success. This scaffolding provides the basis for the unique guided reading formats. As students learn more about the reading process and develop effective reading skills and strategies, the teacher support gradually decreases and students take on more responsibility for their own learning.

What's the Evidence?

The importance of flexible grouping in reading is supported by Au, Carroll, and Scheu, 1997; and by Allington and Walmsley, 1995. Brown, 1999/00; Johnson and Graves, 1996/97; Graves, van den Broek, and Taylor, 1996; Snow, Burns, and Griffin, 1998; and Vygotsky, 1978, 1987 have provided discussions and research on scaffolding and the zone of proximal development and the importance of teaching children at their instructional level.

The importance of placing students at their appropriate instructional level in guided reading is supported by the works of Brown, 1999/00; Johnson and Graves, 1996/97; Fountas and Pinnell, 1996; Graves, van den Broek, and Taylor, 1996; and Vygotsky, 1978, 1987.

The focus for the six guided reading lesson formats is described below.

Early Emergent Stage, Format 1: Concepts of Print (Levels A–B)

The focus of the guided reading lessons for this format is on developing students' awareness of concepts of print. Children at this stage are just beginning to look at letters and words and to attach sounds to letters.

Early Emergent Stage, Format 2: Concepts of Print and Beginning Reading Strategies (Levels C–D)

The format of these guided reading lessons continues to support students' use of concepts of print but more emphasis is placed on developing their ability to use sounds and letters to decode words. Children at this stage are also developing their ability to use a variety of cueing systems when reading.

Upper Emergent Stage, Format 1: Reading Strategies (Levels E–G)

The format of the lesson plan at this stage continues to develop students' ability to use the four cueing systems. There is more emphasis on teaching decoding skills and helping students become proficient in using them.

Upper Emergent Stage, Format 2: Silent Guided Reading (Levels H–J)

By this stage, students are confident in their use of reading strategies. The lessons in this format carefully guide students to read silently for information, to develop comprehension skills, and to integrate reading strategies.

Early Fluency Stage Format: Beginning Literature Circles (Levels K–N)

Students at this stage are consistently using appropriate reading strategies and have good decoding skills. They are ready to read longer text and to begin looking at literary elements and more complex elements of nonfiction. The lessons in this format provide models for developing higher-level comprehension.

Fluency Stage Format: Literature Circles (Levels O–T)

The format for the lessons at the fluency stage are designed to help those students who have nearly mastered the reading process. These students are ready to read longer books, including more chapter books and novels, and to develop a deeper understanding of the literary elements and nonfiction elements found in books.

The Guided Reading Lesson

A guided reading lesson includes three main parts: before, during, and after reading. A summary of each of these parts of the lesson follows. **(See appendix 2 on page 22 for more information on the lesson parts and for a comparison of the six formats.)**

Before Reading

The purpose of the Before Reading segment is to help students prepare for reading. This involves engaging students in discussion to activate any prior knowledge they may have on the topic and to build background knowledge to help them better understand what they are about to read. Students are then asked to make predictions about the book based on the cover illustrations and the title of the book. With a nonfiction book, you can also use the contents page and the index to help students preview the text and make predictions about it.

During Reading

The purpose of the During Reading segment is to give students the opportunity to practice their reading strategies while you observe their reading. Because you are working with a small group of students, it is possible for you to monitor their reading behavior and intervene where necessary. If you notice that a student is having difficulty, you can provide strategy prompts that help students work out unfamiliar words. **(See appendix 3 on page 25 for examples of good strategy prompts for each of the levels.)**

What's the Evidence?

The importance of teaching reading strategies and the correct usage of strategies in the reading process comes from the works of Schwartz, 1997; Goodman, 1996; McIntyre and Pressley, 1996; Tancock, 1994; Garner, 1992; Marlow and Reese, 1992; Richards and Gipe, 1992; and Clay, 1985.

After Reading

The purpose of the After Reading segment is to help students reflect on the reading strategies they used and to consolidate their understanding of the text and its features. Where possible, encourage students to go back to the book to find examples to support their ideas.

Teacher Tips and Think-Alouds

Teacher modeling and intervention strategies are provided where appropriate throughout the lesson in the form of Teacher Tips and Think-Alouds. Teacher Tips suggest activities that can be used to extend students' understanding of the content of the book, to provide background information, or to support the teaching of a skill. Think-Alouds allow you to model for students how to use print conventions, familiar words, known word parts, and the strategies of rereading and self-checking to solve print problems. Think-Alouds also model how to use prediction and questioning in order to understand the text.

What's the Evidence?

The works of Spiegel, 1995 and 1992 support the use of modeling during reading instruction. McNeill, 1992 shows that modeling the thinking process that accompanies reading is an effective way to teach comprehension.

Setting Up Your Classroom

Setting up your classroom for guided reading involves four steps:

- Making sure that your class is ready for small group instruction
- Arranging your room to accommodate small group instruction
- Determining a schedule for meeting with each of your groups
- Having literacy centers in operation

Getting Your Students Ready for Guided Reading

Before you begin your guided reading groups you will want to lay a strong foundation of daily reading and writing activities. This will help ensure that students can independently work in literacy centers and that they are ready for focused small group instruction. Following are activities that will help lay this foundation.

- Shared reading, songs, read-alouds, paired reading, and independent reading
- Talking about stories with others
- Responding to stories through reproductions, innovations, retellings, dramatic reenactments, and other artistic creations
- Reading familiar stories independently or with a partner
- Writing in a variety of formats, such as stories, journals, diaries, letters, and logs
- Working on Daily News activities and other written language experiences

Preparing Your Classroom

You will probably want to have a specific area for guided reading sessions, as well as other areas in the classroom to accommodate your literacy centers. These simple steps will help ensure the success of your guided reading program.

- Set aside a specific area for meeting with your small guided reading groups. You might arrange yourself and the students together at a table or on the floor, or you may prefer to sit on a chair with the children sitting in front of you in a semicircle on the floor.

- Position yourself so that you can observe the entire classroom as you conduct guided reading groups.
- Keep your guided reading books in a convenient location for easy access.
- Have a chalkboard, pocket chart, magnetic boards, magnetic letters, sentence strips, pencils, markers, paper, and other supplies in the area for skill instruction.
- Arrange your quietest literacy centers closest to your guided reading area and the more interactive centers farther away.

Your Guided Reading Schedule

During a typical day in your classroom you will probably be able to meet with three to four guided reading groups during your reading time. Each guided reading group will require approximately fifteen to twenty minutes of instructional time. If you have more than three or four groups you may only be able to meet with each group three to four times a week instead of every day. However, you should try to meet with your early emergent groups on a daily basis to ensure that they are getting a strong foundation in reading. If you have students that are reading below grade level, you may also wish to meet with those students every day but for a longer period of time, approximately thirty minutes, to provide the additional support in reading, writing, and skill and strategy instruction that they require.

Setting Up Literacy Centers in Your Classroom

Literacy centers provide opportunities for students to work cooperatively with a partner or small group, or independently, while practicing and applying the skills and strategies that they learn during guided reading lessons. Students can work at different literacy centers while you work with your guided reading groups.

The most appropriate centers to develop reading and writing skills are reading centers, integrated language arts centers, skill centers, and desk centers.

Reading centers include the Big Book center, poetry center, library center, pocket chart center, overhead center, read-the-room center, and book boxes center.

Integrated language arts centers include the writing and publishing center, listening center, drama and/or music center, and computer center.

Skill centers are centers such as the alphabet center, word study center, and word walls.

Desk centers provide opportunities for reading independently, doing extension activities from the guided reading lesson, creating and using graphic organizers, and playing word or letter games.

At the beginning of the year you will want to allow plenty of time for students to become familiar with working at centers. For some students this may take several weeks. Once students learn how to manage their time and activities at centers, they can function quite independently, giving you the time to meet with each of your guided reading groups.

Managing Your Classroom: A Practical Example

Class Profile

There are twenty-two students in this example of a first-grade classroom. The students are at these levels:

- Four students are reading Level C books at an early emergent level
- Five students are reading Level E books at an upper emergent level
- Ten students are reading Level F books at an upper emergent level
- Three students are reading Level L books at an early fluency level

Guided Reading Groups

There will need to be five guided reading groups in this class. The group of ten reading Level F books is too large for one group and will have to be split.

Schedule

There is an hour and twenty minutes scheduled for guided reading from 8:55–10:15. The group reading books at Level C should have a guided reading lesson every day since they are below grade level. This may take more than the fifteen to twenty minutes regularly scheduled for groups and include more intensive skill and strategy instruction. The group reading Level L books is above grade level and may have a guided reading lesson only two to three times in a week. The following chart shows how a guided reading schedule might look in this particular classroom.

Group	Time	M	T	W	Th	F
C	8:55–9:20	X	X	X	X	X
E	9:20–9:40	X	X	X	X	X
F	9:40–10:00		X	X	X	X
F	10:00–10:15	X		X		X
L	10:00–10:15		X		X	

What Are the Rest of Your Students Doing?

As you are meeting with group E, for example, the other students are either at literacy centers or at their seats. Students from group C may be working at the word study center practicing high-frequency words. Students in the first group of those reading books at Level F may be in the library center and the Big Book center reading books. Students in the second group of those reading books at Level F may be reading independently or with a partner from their book boxes and be found either at their seats or in comfortable spots around the room. Students from group L may be completing graphic organizers at their seats.

When you change guided reading groups, the students working at literacy centers will move to another center. You may wish to create some type of management chart so students know which center they should move to. You may also wish to have their center selections be free choice. An example of an easy management system is to create a large chart listing all of your literacy centers. You may attach self-fastening fabric tape to each section of the chart and to cards that list each of your groups. The chart can then quickly be set up each day during your opening activities with students to ensure that they know what is expected of them during guided reading time.

For more on centers and setting up your classroom, see *The Story Box Resource Guide* from the *Story Box Reading Program* by the Wright Group.

Placing Your Students in Appropriate Groups

Prior to forming guided reading groups, you will need to assess each student's reading level and determine what strategies and skills you need to focus on. Any of the assessments mentioned below will assist you in placing students at their correct reading level.

Assessment of Reading Behavior

An Assessment of Reading Behavior is the most effective means of placing students at an appropriate instructional reading level. It is also a means to continue monitoring students' reading to ensure that they are always reading at the correct level. This tool assesses the reading strategies and skills that students are using as they interact with text. By analyzing an Assessment of Reading Behavior, you can determine if students are reading a particular book at an instructional reading level (90 to 94 percent), at an independent reading level (95 to 100 percent), or at a too difficult reading level (below 90 percent). This tool also provides information to guide your instruction.

Once you have placed a student at the correct instructional reading level, you need to continually monitor that student's reading behavior. If after a few days the student consistently reads the books at a particular level with 90 to 94 percent accuracy, you need to consider moving that student up a level to slightly more difficult books.

An Assessment of Reading Behavior is an ongoing assessment of students' reading behavior and the development of their skills. This assessment should be conducted at regular intervals to monitor reading behaviors. For example, use the assessment:

- At the beginning of the year to establish baseline reading information
- At the end of each set of guided reading books
- Quarterly and at the end of the school year
- At least weekly or even daily with students requiring extra support
- When students appear ready to accelerate to the next instructional reading level

As part of guided reading each day, you may wish to select one student in each group for an Assessment of Reading Behavior. By the end of a week, you will have a reading assessment on most of the children in your classroom. **(A blank Assessment of Reading Behavior form is included in appendix 6 on pages 30 and 31 and can be used with any book at any time.)**

Administering an Assessment of Reading Behavior

On the front of the Assessment of Reading Behavior, record the results of the student's reading, evaluate his or her retelling of the story, and determine an overall level of the student's proficiency. Using this assessment involves five steps:

1. Selecting the Text

2. Reading and Recording

3. Checking Comprehension and Skills

4. Scoring the Reading

5. Analyzing the Results

Selecting the Text

The text or book that you select for an Assessment of Reading Behavior will depend on your reason for using this assessment and the instructional level of the student.

Text for this type of an assessment is either "seen text" or "unseen text." At the early emergent level, when students are just learning to use reading strategies and behaviors, you may wish to use seen text, or text that they are already familiar with. Once students have developed some reading strategies and can use these strategies to decode unknown words, you may, on occasion, choose an unseen, or new, text to assess their reading.

Use Seen Text
- To monitor student progress and instructional level on a regular basis
- To evaluate use of reading cues and strategies
- To determine lesson and/or skill focus
- To monitor reading group placements
- To evaluate comprehension
- To evaluate how student approaches familiar text
- To provide long-term documentation of reading behaviors

- To evaluate the independent use of strategies and how well students process unknown text
- To determine instructional reading level
- To determine student's readiness to move to next reading level
- To evaluate student's willingness to take risks
- To evaluate student's comprehension of unfamiliar text
- To provide long-term documentation of reading behaviors

Reading and Recording

During this part of the assessment, you introduce the book and then have the student read the selected text while you record his or her reading behaviors.

Introducing the Book

It is important that the student has a general understanding of the story before reading it to help connect meaning to what he or she reads. If the student has already read the book (seen text), just say the title of the book. If the book has not been read by the child (unseen text), read the title of the book and then provide a brief introduction summarizing the story, for example, "This story is about some bears that go on a picnic."

Recording the Reading

Ask the child to read the book aloud to you independently. Let the student know you will not help unless the student is really stuck on a word. Sit close enough to observe the student reading. As he or she reads, record all of the student's reading behaviors on the back of the Assessment of Reading Behavior form.

If the student pauses or stops reading, do not prompt. Allow plenty of time for the student to use his or her reading strategies to figure out a tricky or difficult word before you jump in to help. It is important, however, not to wait too long as the student may lose the meaning of the story. If a student is really stuck, your first prompt should be "You try it," "What could it be?" or something similar.

An Assessment of Reading Behavior can be done with a book of any length. A realistic reading sample is from 100 to 150 words. Many of the books at the early emergent and upper emergent levels contain fewer than 100 words, so you will want the student to read the entire book. If a book has more than 100 words, have the student stop reading at an appropriate point, such as at the end of a paragraph or at the end of a page.

If a student omits a line on a page while reading, count each word skipped as an error. If the student skips a whole page, however, by turning two pages at once, deduct the number of words on that page from the total word count.

At times students may encounter a difficult proper noun (personal or place name) and consistently miscue on it. These miscues are counted as one error only, regardless of the number of times the proper noun is misread. If other words in a story are repeated several times and the student miscues each time he or she attempts the word, each miscued word is counted as an error.

To assess how a student is reading, you will be using a series of notations that indicate what behaviors students are using as they read. See the notations in the Reading Behavior Notations chart that follows.

Reading Behavior Notations

Notation	Behavior	How to Use Notation	Example	Error	Self-Correction
√	Correct response	Check the correct response.	√ √ √ √ √ I can see the flowers.	0	0
came can	Substitution	Write the response over the text.	√ **came** √ √ √ I can see the flowers.	1	0
can	Omission	Circle the omitted word.	√ √ √ √ I can see the flowers.	1	0
pretty –	Insertion	Insert the added word above the text.	√ √ √ √ **pretty** √ I can see the flowers.	1	0
f---	Letter cues	Show sounds tried.	√ √ √ √ **f - -** I can see the flowers.	1	0
↓ R	Repetition	Write R and show the words repeated.	√ √ √ √ **R** √ I can see the flowers.	0	0
see/SC	Self-correction	Write SC after a corrected error.	√ √ **smell/sc** √ √ I can see the flowers.	0	1
A see	Asks for help	Write A over the word asked for.	√ √ **A** √ √ I can see the flowers.	0	0
T see	Teacher supplies word	Write T over words that you supply.	√ √ **T** √ √ I can see the flowers.	1	0
f-f-fl-flowers flowers	Successfully attempts word	Write the attempts over the word.	√ √ √ √ **f-f-fl-flowers** √ I can see the flowers.	0	0
f-f-friends flowers	Unsuccessfully attempts word	Write the attempts over the word.	√ √ √ √ **f-f-friends** I can see the flowers.	1	0

Checking Comprehension and Skills

After the child finishes reading the book, or the first 100 to 150 word selection, you may either ask the student to retell the story or ask him or her comprehension questions about the story. You may at times wish to ask students to do both the retelling and the comprehension check.

Retelling

Ask the student to retell the story in his or her own words. If necessary, prompt the student to tell you more about the characters, setting, and/or events. On the front of the Assessment of Reading Behavior form, record the information about the retelling strategies the student used and if the retelling was prompted or not. Score the student's comments about characters, setting, and events by noting whether the retelling showed complete, adequate, or limited understanding of the story.

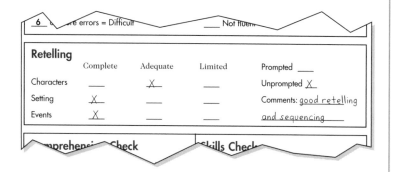

Comprehension Check

If you wish to do a more in-depth evaluation of the student's level of comprehension and understanding of skills, use the Comprehension Check section on the Assessment of Reading Behavior form.

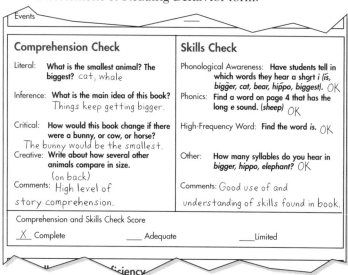

This part of the Assessment of Reading Behavior form allows you to enter your own questions to monitor comprehension. It prompts you to ask questions that evaluate three levels of comprehension and provide one activity that elicits a creative reaction to the story.

- **Literal questions**—Answers to these questions can be found in the text. These questions ask the student to recall specific information about the story, for example: "Where did the bears go on their picnic?"

- **Inference questions**—These questions require that the student draw on prior knowledge and experience in addition to using information from the book to think about the story's meaning, for example: "What else could the bears have taken on their picnic?"

- **Critical questions**—These questions require the student to evaluate critically the meaning of a story and his or her own understanding of a story before making decisions about an event or character, for example: "Was it okay for the little boy to wave at everyone? Why or why not?"

- **Creative response**—This activity encourages the student to respond creatively to the story. For example, invite the student to illustrate a part of the story or draw the characters, dramatize a part of the story, write a new ending, or write an innovation. You may choose to do this activity only occasionally and not with every book on which you take an assessment.

Skills Check

The Skills Check section provides opportunities to focus on the students' understanding and use of skills in the following areas:

- **Phonological Awareness**—These questions focus on the student's ability to hear rhymes, hear sounds, blend and segment words orally, and form new words by changing the onset/rimes.

- **Phonics**—These questions address the student's ability to make sound-symbol associations and recognize word families and vowel patterns.

- **High-Frequency Word**—These questions direct the student to identify a high-frequency word in the story.

- **Other**—Use this category to ask questions about word families, rhyming words, words with plural endings, contractions, multisyllabic words, and so on in the story.

Score the Comprehension Check and Skills Check sections as follows:

- **Complete**—Student successfully answers all comprehension and skill questions correctly.
- **Adequate**—Student answers most comprehension and/or skill questions correctly.
- **Limited**—Student answers few or none of the comprehension and/or skill questions correctly.

See page 12 for how to determine an overall reading level using the comprehension scores.

Scoring the Reading

Score the assessment as soon as possible after taking the Assessment of Reading Behavior so as to not overlook or forget the student's behaviors.

Determining the Error Rate and Accuracy

To determine the error rate and accuracy of the assessment, complete the following steps:

1. Count the number of errors in each line of the assessment and record the total in the "E" column on the Assessment of Reading Behavior form. **(See appendix 6 on page 30.)**

2. Count the total number of errors in the "E" column.

3. To determine the error rate, divide the number of words read by the total number of errors. For example, 70 words read divided by 4 errors equals 17.5 (70/4 = 17.5).

4. Use the Error and Accuracy Rates chart **(see appendix 7 on page 31)** to determine the accuracy rate and the corresponding reading level. For example, if a student has an error rate of 1:17.5, look on the chart under "Error Rate" for that rate. Read across the chart for the corresponding accuracy rate (rounded to the next highest number), which is "95%." Then determine the reading level, which is "independent."

5. Record this information on the front of the Assessment of Reading Behavior form in the "Scoring" section.

Assessment of Reading Behavior: Set D

Scoring:

Words __49__ = Error Rate 1: __12__   Accuracy Rate __92__ %   SC Rate 1: __2__
Errors __4__

Reading Level: ____ Independent   __X__ Instructional   ____ Difficult
Seen text __X__   Unseen text ____

For this title:	Reading Fluency
__0__ to __2__ errors = Independent	____ Fluent
__3__ to __5__ errors = Instructional	__X__ Word by word
__6__ or more errors = Difficult	____ Not fluent

Determining the Self-Correction Rate

Self-corrections are positive reading behaviors and are not counted as errors. Follow these steps for determining self-correction rates:

1. Count the number of self-corrections on each line and record the numbers in the "SC" column on the assessment form.

2. Count the total number of self-corrections in the "SC" column.

3. Add the total number of errors to the total number of self-corrections. Then divide the resulting sum by the total number of self-corrections, for example: 4 total errors made plus 2 self-corrections equals 6. Divide 6 by the total number of self-corrections (2) for an answer of 3. [(4 + 2)/2 = 6/2 = 3] The self-correction rate is recorded as 1:3, which means that the student corrected one time for every 3 words that were misread. A self-correction rate of 1:3 to 1:5 is considered good; a rate of 1:2 is excellent. Even a poor self-correction rate of 1:7 or higher shows that the student is beginning to pay attention to the text and to use decoding strategies.

4. Record this information on the front of the Assessment of Reading Behavior form in the "Scoring" section.

Analyzing the Results

The final step in effectively using the Assessment of Reading Behavior is to analyze how the student performed and what cues, strategies, and behaviors he or she was using while reading.

1. Think about what might have caused the child to make the error. Try to determine if the student was using meaning (semantic) cues, structure (syntactic) cues, or visual (graphophonic) cues up to the point of the miscue. Meaning, or semantic, cues are those based on the context of the story. Structure, or syntactic, cues are those based on the grammar, syntax, or language structure. Graphophonic cues are those based on visual information and/or phonics cues.

2. In the column labeled "Cues Used—Errors" check the cues (M, S, V) that the student was using when the error was made.

3. To analyze the use of self-correction strategies, think about what might have caused the student to make the error in the first place and then consider what he or she did to correct the error.

4. In the column labeled "Cues Used—Self-Corrections," check the cues that were used to self-correct the errors.

5. Analyze the types and number of cues the student used at the point of the error and what he or she did to self-correct. To decode successfully, students should be using all cues nearly equally and not overrelying on the use of one cue. If a student relies on one cue consistently, you will need to focus your instruction on using all of the cueing systems.

Analyzing Reading Behaviors

Reading Behaviors	Questions to ask yourself
Substitution	Why do you think the child chose that particular word? Was it visually similar to the written word? Did it fit in grammatically?
Omission	Why do you think the child changed the text? Was it grammatically correct with the omission?
Insertion	Why do you think the child inserted that word? Was the text grammatically correct with the insertion?
Letter Cues	Is sounding out enough of a clue? Is the child able to use any other strategy to help? Were individual letters used/blended? Did the child use syllables, word families, or phrases?
Repetition	What do you think might have caused the child to go back and repeat that part? What word was next?
Self-Correction	What caught the child's attention and caused him or her to self-correct?

Determining Overall Reading Proficiency

Use the reading level from the Error and Accuracy Rates chart and the level of comprehension to summarize a student's performance in the "Overall Reading Proficiency" section on the front of the Assessment of Reading Behavior form. For example, if a student read a book with 94 percent accuracy and had an Adequate score on comprehension, his or her overall reading proficiency on that book would be at the Instructional level.

(Use the chart in appendix 7 on page 31 to help you determine an overall reading proficiency.)

Assessment of Reading Behavior

		Cues Used*					
		Errors			Self-Corrections		
	M	S	V	M	S	V	Comments
	✓	✓					Natural language with Kitty. Not looking at word endings.
	✓		✓				
	✓	✓				✓	Looked at whole word.
	✓	✓					Not looking at word endings.
	✓	✓				✓	Looked at word to SC.
	✓		✓				
	✓	✓		✓	✓		Looked at word ending.

Informing Instruction

An Assessment of Reading Behavior will help you clearly see the cues, strategies, and behaviors that students are using as they process and decode text. Use the information from this assessment to help you determine the skills and reading strategies in which students need instruction and support.

Once you have an Assessment of Reading Behavior on each of your students at the beginning of the school year, you can place students at the correct instructional level in guided reading groups. By continuing to give the assessment at regular intervals, you can monitor students' reading development and placement and determine whether to move students to a higher or lower group or to provide more support in their current reading group.

Overall Reading Proficiency

Reading Level __Instructional__ + Comprehension & Skills Score __Complete__ = Reading Proficiency Score

__X__ Independent ____ Instructional ____ Difficult

Comments: Amanda has good story comprehension. She is really starting to pay more attention to whole words but needs to continue practicing looking through words.

Other Assessments

You may also use additional assessments to help you determine placement of students in guided reading groups. Some of the areas you might want to assess include:

- Phonological awareness to evaluate how well students hear sounds in language

- Concepts of print to determine if students have an understanding of print features, book and text concepts, one-to-one correspondence, and directionality

- Letter recognition and reproduction to identify what letters students know and can reproduce

- Phonics to evaluate whether students can make connections between sounds and symbols

- High-frequency words to determine which high-frequency words students can readily identify

Monitoring students' growth in reading development, ongoing assessments, and daily observations are critical components in a successful reading program. These assessments allow you to regroup students when necessary to teach specific skills that have been identified or to move a student to another level when necessary.

Guided reading time provides a perfect opportunity to assess your students' reading behaviors, skills development, appropriate reading level, and comprehension skills. Working with a small group of two to five students makes it much easier to observe and monitor how each student is handling print.

As you observe students during guided reading, you can use a variety of checklists or anecdotal notes to record their reading behaviors. Independent reading time at the end of each guided reading session is also an ideal opportunity to take an Assessment of Reading Behavior on one child in each group each day. By continually monitoring and assessing students you are always aware of their instructional needs and can effectively plan your lessons to best meet their needs.

For more on assessment see the Wright Group's *The Story Box Reading Program Assessment Guide* for Early Emergent and Upper Emergent, *SUNSHINE Assessment Guide* for Grades K-1, *Sunshine Assessment Guide* for Grades 2-3, and *The Wright Skills Assessment Guide*.

What's the Evidence?

The importance of ongoing assessments that address the needs of students and inform instruction is supported by Cheyney and Cohen, 1999; Strickland, 1998; Tierney, 1998; Au, Carroll, and Scheu, 1997; Christie, Enz, and Vukelich, 1997; Fountas and Pinnell, 1996; Cunningham, 1995; and Herman, Aschbacher, and Winters, 1993.

Frequent use of a wide range of assessments to address the needs of all students is supported by Cheyney and Cohen, 1999; Glazer, 1998; Tierney, 1998; West, 1998; Braunger and Lewis, 1997; Calfee, 1996; Graves, van den Broek, and Taylor, 1996; Harp, 1996; Cunningham, 1995; and Clay, 1993.

Choosing the Right Books

The books that you use for guided reading will typically be small books that contain one story and are generally eight to thirty-two pages long. At the early fluency and fluency stages, books increase in length and may even include some chapter books. The books should be ones that students have not seen yet so that they can use their reading strategies to decode and comprehend new material.

When matching students to books, you need to consider the number of pages, number of words, number of lines per page, and number of words per sentence, as well as the book features, such as difficult vocabulary, sentence structure and syntax, illustration support, and text support. You need to also consider the students' characteristics, abilities, and prior knowledge.

The importance of matching students to books that support their instructional reading level has already been mentioned. Students should be able to read approximately 90 to 94 percent of the words in the book. These books should be challenging enough to require students to develop and use their reading strategies and skills but not so difficult that they become frustrated in their reading. It is not necessary for students to read every book within a level. Once your students have read several books at a level with 90 to 94 percent accuracy, it is time to consider moving them up to the next level.

You should try to provide a variety of books within a level in order to select the books most appropriate for students' instructional needs and interests. You will also want to include a variety of genres, including fiction and nonfiction. This variety will enable your guided reading groups to be more flexible since you will be able to pick books that match the students' needs.

When students have finished reading a book, that book should be placed in either an individual or group book box. These books can then be used during literacy center time or during independent reading time. As students reread their books at an independent level they develop fluency, automaticity, and confidence.

Using Nonfiction Books for Guided Reading

Children are naturally drawn to nonfiction as they encounter and explore the world around them. A guided reading lesson built around nonfiction materials can provide the reading-to-learn portion of a balanced reading program, and help children understand how to locate and extract information from nonfiction texts.

The purpose of nonfiction is to present information that informs, instructs, enlightens, or persuades the reader. This information is provided through the text as well as through visual elements, such as charts, maps, diagrams, photographs, captions, labels, and drawings. In addition, many nonfiction books are organized to contain a table of contents, index, glossary, and chapter headings and subheadings. Children need to learn how to derive meaning from these various components of a nonfiction book. They also need to learn how to read these books critically. Nonfiction is supposedly a representation of accurate information that is presented in an objective way. However, it is written from the perspective of a writer who has a particular point of view and may not always be objective in nature. Through guided reading lessons with nonfiction text, teachers can ensure that their students are equipped with the skills and knowledge to extract information and interpret it in a critical way.

The Guided Reading Process with Nonfiction Books

The process for using nonfiction books in guided reading is the same as the process for using fiction books. You will still follow the same steps for before, during, and after reading. What does vary are the questioning strategies and modeling that you might do with nonfiction material. You will need to ask probing questions and ask for predictions that will help students discover answers or arouse their curiosity. You will need to encourage them to seek information that will help them make, confirm, and revise their predictions as they read. Through the modeling in the Think-Alouds and the Visual Learning sections of the guided reading lessons, you will help students come to understand how to interpret the various components of nonfiction texts and encourage them to think critically about the content.

Following are some suggestions for developing nonfiction reading strategies during the guided reading process.

Before Reading

Build Background: Ask questions that draw on students' prior knowledge to help them develop a better understanding of the content. Use graphic organizers, such as KWHL or KWL charts, word webs, and lists, as well as additional photos, videos, Internet searches, and articles whenever possible.

Introduce the Book: Ask questions that focus on nonfiction elements and text features, such as the table of contents, glossary, captions, and strategies for using these features when applicable. The purpose of focusing on these text features is to help students learn previewing skills that they will later be able to transfer to independent reading situations. Students need to learn to make decisions about the text and information presented in a book in order to determine if a particular text is appropriate for their needs.

During Reading

Focus the Reading: Your questions should encourage students to find evidence to support a fact, read to confirm information, find the topic sentence, make inferences, find information that reinforces what they already know, find a definition for a term, analyze how ideas are connected, and so on.

After Reading

Build Comprehension: You will want to ask questions that help students focus on the content and the nonfiction elements of the book. Questions might include those which help students locate important details; summarize the main idea; evaluate the content; determine the author's purpose; evaluate the accuracy of the information presented; understand tables, graphs, maps; analyze the information; compare information; confirm understandings; and so on. You may also wish to use graphic organizers to record information from the book as well as record information that reflects students' learning.

Graphic Organizers

Students may also create their own visual representations to organize their thinking and to record what they have learned. These help students verbally and visually summarize and depict their learning. These graphic organizers provide useful ways to facilitate discussions, motivate learning, actively involve students, and help them organize new information. Some examples of graphic organizers follow:

- **KWL or KWHL charts**—recording what students know about a topic, what they want to learn (how they will find out), and what they have learned
- **Feature Analysis Charts**—comparing and contrasting various characteristics of a topic or concept
- **Graphs, charts, diagrams**—visually recording or showing information
- **Venn diagrams**—showing similarities and differences between two or more objects, concepts, or ideas
- **Sequence charts and time lines**—showing a sequence of events or the chronological order of events
- **Information webs and word webs**—organizing and sorting information into different categories or creating a visual representation of a concept
- **Problem/solutions/effects matrix**—showing a problem being addressed; the solution or possible solutions; and what effects the problem and/or solution have on people, animals, and the environment

Once students have completed their own graphic organizer, it is useful to have them write a summary statement of what they have learned from the organizational process. When children are able to generalize or summarize their learning, they are using higher-level thinking strategies and are becoming more capable learners and users of nonfiction text.

Criteria for Leveling Books at the Early Emergent Stage

Criteria	Levels: Pre-A, A, and B	Student Outcomes
Book Features	• number of pages: 8 • number of words: generally less than 40 • number of lines per page: 1–2 • number of words per sentence: range of 2–7; average 5	**Level Pre-A** • Hears syllables in words • Hears and uses rhyming words • Repeats the alphabet • Identifies and names some letters • Knows how to handle a book properly • Is beginning to track print left to right • Attends to approximately 5 high-frequency words
Text Features	• well-spaced large print • consistent text placement • some use of return sweep • cover and title page integral to book • some variety of punctuation	
Illustration Features	• one illustration per page • direct match of text and illustrations • objects clearly defined • illustrations tell the story and reinforce left-right progression • illustrations are highly supportive	**Levels A-B** • Orally segments and blends some words • Orally uses onset/rime to create new words • Identifies initial sounds in spoken words
Language and Sentence Features	• repetition of high-frequency words and sentence structure • most content words familiar • 1–2 word changes per page • natural language structures • simple language patterns	• Hears and produces rhyming sounds • Knows the sound of most letters • Recognizes that illustrations and books tell a story or relate information • Has acquired many concepts of print (word/space/sentence, return sweep, one-to-one correspondence)
Story Features	• highly predictable story line • generally complete sentences • structure may change on last page • stories have a simple beginning, middle, and ending • surprise endings or twists • familiar concepts	• Recognizes that print contains meaning • Identifies and names most letters • Reads approx. 5–10 high-frequency words • Locates known words within text • Predicts story events • Has a sense of story

Criteria	Levels: C and D	Student Outcomes
Book Features	• number of pages: generally 8, some 12–16 • number of words: generally less than 70 • number of lines per page: 1–4 • number of words per sentence: range 2–8; average 6	• Uses phonological awareness skills of syllable awareness, rhyme awareness, onset/rime, and blending and segmenting sounds • Identifies most medial and final sounds in spoken words • Knows book concepts of cover, title page, author, illustrator • Has developed text concepts of picture, sentence, punctuation, capitalization • Has developed word concepts of directionally and one-to-one correspondence • Knows all letter names and primary sounds • Uses initial letter/sound to decode • Uses short vowel sounds to decode • Recognizes that some letters make more than one sound • Uses word families to build words and decode • Identifies approx. 18–20 high-frequency words • Uses beginning reading strategies (self-correction) • Identifies character, setting, problem/solution in story • Is able to sequence a story • Recalls some details from book • Retells story or summarizes information
Text Features	• placement of text may vary • frequent use of return sweep • wide range of punctuation • ample space between words • some captions with phrases in nonfiction books • question and answer format in nonfiction books • some use of graphic organizers in nonfiction books	
Illustration Features	• one illustration per page or spread • illustrations depict only some or much of the text • clearly defined objects • illustrations are supportive, but emphasis is on text • story line found in text as well as illustrations	
Language and Sentence Features	• repetition of familiar and unfamiliar high-frequency words • some unfamiliar content words • variations in sentence structure • some use of direct speech • 2–3 or more word changes per page • phrases or patterns repeated • some use of past tense, inflected endings (-ing, -ed, -s) • some compound words • some multisyllabic words	
Story Features	• text is less predicable but supported by meaning and sentence structure • sentence structure may be somewhat complex and change on last page or on every few pages • surprise endings or twists • familiar concepts	

Criteria for Leveling Books at the Upper Emergent Stage

Criteria	Levels: E, F, and G	Student Outcomes
Book Features	• number of pages: 8–16 • number of words: less than 180 • number of lines per page: generally 2–4 with some more than 4 • number of words per sentence: range 4–15; average 10	• Uses phonological awareness skills of blending, segmenting, and manipulating sounds in words • Can determine number of sounds heard in spoken words • Is able to blend letter sounds to decode • Uses letter/sound correspondence to decode • Knows several word families • Uses medial and final sounds to decode • Is able to decode some one-sound letter combinations (*ch*, *th*) • Tries more than one sound of a letter to decode • Knows many vowel patterns and uses these in decoding • Uses knowledge of compound words to decode • Uses known word parts to decode • Is beginning to integrate reading strategies • Knows approx. 50–100 high-frequency words • Recognizes plurals • Reads to gain meaning from print • Recognizes story sequence • Is gaining more understanding of character, setting, problem/solution
Text Features	• print reduced to medium sized • variety of placement of text • wide range of punctuation • table of contents, glossary, index, captions with phrases and/or sentences in nonfiction • frequent use of graphic organizers/diagrams • question and answer format common in nonfiction books	
Illustration Features	• one per page or spread • provide moderate support • often very detailed • text carries more meaning than illustrations • suggest sequence of events • provide information about characters, setting, events • used to confirm and support text and inform the reader	
Language and Sentence Features	• expanded use of high-frequency words • many high-frequency words introduced and reinforced • challenging vocabulary • variety in syntax and word tenses • some multisyllabic and compound words used • use of descriptive and literary language • often requires use of context for meaning • 4 or more word changes and/or entire pattern changes • sentences may carry over to next page • some compound sentences • dialogue mixed with prose • written language patterns instead of oral language patterns	
Story Features	• moderately complex story structures with problem/solution emphasized • structure in book may change 2–3 times or on every page • clear story line and sequence of events • events continue throughout book and over more than one page • requires higher-level comprehension strategies and use of inference • characters and events increasingly developed • topics generally familiar but increasing in complexity	

Criteria	Levels: H, I, and J	Student Outcomes
Book Features	• number of pages: generally 16–24 • number of words: less than 300 • number of lines per page: average 3–8 • number of words per sentence: range 4–18; average 12	• Uses letter-sound correspondence to decode unknown words • Uses word chunks to decode • Decodes most words with vowel patterns • Knows some words are spelled the same but sound different • Is developing automaticity in recognizing high-frequency words • Integrates reading strategies • Rereads for meaning • Uses context to determine meaning • Determines main idea of simple text • Makes inferences to gain meaning • Is beginning to understand literary elements of character, setting, cause/effect, problem/solution • Is developing fluency in reading • Reads silently for information and meaning • Uses table of contents, index, glossary • Skims familiar text to locate literal information • Compares similar texts • Maintains meaning in longer texts
Text Features	• print size may vary from medium to small • variety of font and text placement • extra space between paragraphs • chapter heads in nonfiction • frequent use of graphic organizers in nonfiction • photos, illustrations, and captions in nonfiction often very detailed and may fill entire page	
Illustration Features	• generally one per spread • illustrations are detailed and provide moderate to minimal support • used to confirm and support text and inform reader • used to create interest • detailed illustrations depict characters, setting, and events instead of specific details	
Language and Sentence Features	• frequent use of known and unknown high-frequency words • high-frequency words occur naturally in text • challenging and specialized vocabulary • multisyllabic words common • vocabulary may require use of context to determine meaning • ample familiar vocabulary to promote fluency • frequent use of compound words • use of descriptive and literary language • dialogue mixed with prose • some technical vocabulary in nonfiction • complex structure with compound sentences	
Story Features	• limited repetition and predictability • complex story structure and story line • several episodes in one book • continuation of events over several pages • character descriptions are involved • points of view found in story • sequential passages that detail why something happened or how it was done • variety of text features and genres	

Criteria for Leveling Books at the Early Fluency Stage

Criteria	Levels: K, L, M, and N	Student Outcomes
Book Features	• number of pages: 16–24 • number of words: less than 600 • number of lines per page: usually 1/2 to full page of text • number of words per sentence: range 4–26; average 14	• Uses phonics and word analysis skills to decode • Recognizes and uses several complex letter-sound relationships • Identifies meaning of many words using root words and affixes • Uses knowledge of antonyms and synonyms to predict words • Identifies meaning of most unknown words using context • Reads for meaning • Uses multiple-reading strategies • Uses problem-solving strategies on unknown words • Self-monitors reading • Rereads to monitor reading strategies • Uses story context to cross-check • Cross-checks one strategy with another • Predicts and confirms predictions • Determines main idea • Summarizes and/or paraphrases short stories or paragraphs • Has developed independence in reading • Reads aloud fluently • Recognizes many literary elements and is able to interpret text • Infers author's meaning from text • Reads a variety of genres
Text Features	• decreased print size • less space between words • paragraphs are set off with some paragraphs indented • use of some chapter books • captions in nonfiction range from single word to compound sentences • italics used for new terms in nonfiction • wide variety of graphic organizers in nonfiction	
Illustration Features	• one per spread and often not full page • extend and support the text and enhance plot • used to create interest • some use of line drawings to create interest • not used to depict specific details or concepts • mix of illustrations, photos, diagrams, graphs, etc. in nonfiction	
Language and Sentence Features	• naturally occurring high-frequency words • more challenging high-frequency words introduced • specialized vocabulary imbedded into text • descriptive and challenging vocabulary • use of literary language • use of idioms, similes, metaphors • complex sentence structures • frequent use of multiple phrases in one sentence • dialogue is prevalent	
Story Features	• predictability based on events and content • complex sequences and events • well-developed story lines • character descriptions apparent and detailed • character development is key to story • characters and plots are becoming fully developed and interactive • conflict/resolution introduced • many episodes built around single plot • inference required to predict events • complex story structures • complex plots • details are important to story • abstract themes may be used • details and literary elements key to story line • wide variety of text features and genres	

Criteria for Leveling Books at the Fluency Stage

Criteria	Levels: O, P, Q, R, S, and T	Student Outcomes
Book Features	<ul><li>number of pages: 24–48</li><li>number of words: n/a</li><li>number of lines per page: full page of text</li><li>number of words per sentence: average 16 with some longer</li></ul>	<ul><li>Recognizes and uses most complex letter-sound relationships</li><li>Uses structural analysis skills to decode unknown words; i.e. syllabication, root words, prefixes, suffixes, synonyms, antonyms, and so on</li><li>Analyzes unknown words by using word chunks, letter clusters, prefixes, suffixes, root words, etc.</li><li>Has developed automaticity in using and integrating reading strategies</li><li>Skims unfamiliar text for information</li><li>Retains meaning of complex sentences</li><li>Summarizes and/or paraphrases complex passages or texts</li><li>Understands idioms, similes, and figurative language</li><li>Analyzes problems and relationships between characters</li><li>Compares and contrasts genres, text features, themes</li><li>Identifies mood, tone, theme</li><li>Analyzes fact/opinion, quality of source, etc.</li><li>Locates inferred ideas/messages in text</li><li>Responds to, understands, and analyzes literature elements and nonfiction features</li><li>Uses critical thinking, inference, and problem-solving strategies to develop comprehension</li><li>Reads a variety of genres</li><li>Has developed fluency in reading</li><li>Reads text independently for information and enjoyment</li></ul>
Text Features	<ul><li>longer and more developed paragraphs and sections</li><li>paragraphs usually indented</li><li>decreased print size</li><li>expanded story lines</li><li>many chapter books with two facing pages of text</li><li>captions may be full page with illustrations/photos</li></ul>	
Illustration Features	<ul><li>generally one per spread</li><li>provide limited support, are used to create interest, enhance meaning, and convey information</li><li>specific details or concepts not always illustrated</li><li>mix of photos, illustrations, and graphic organizers on single spread in nonfiction</li><li>in chapter books 1/4 to 1/2 page and often only few per book</li><li>occasional use of full spread for maps, diagrams, etc.</li></ul>	
Language and Sentence Features	<ul><li>challenging high-frequency words occur naturally in text</li><li>prepositional phrases often at beginning of sentences</li><li>use of descriptive and figurative language with elaboration and details</li><li>use of multiple meaning words</li><li>vocabulary with strong imagery</li><li>integrated literary language</li><li>clearly defined terms</li><li>formal dialogue</li><li>varied syntax</li><li>complex sentence and language structures</li><li>multiple phrases in one sentence</li></ul>	
Story Features	<ul><li>predictability based on events and content</li><li>well-developed story structure</li><li>inference required to predict story line</li><li>comprehensive development of literary elements</li><li>well-developed and dynamic characters</li><li>complex characters and events</li><li>many new and unfamiliar concepts</li><li>details found in text</li><li>sophisticated themes</li><li>variety of genres</li></ul>	

Lesson Steps

Format 1: Early Emergent, Concepts of Print

- During **Picture Walk**, teacher uses pictures to involve students in discussion about book. Vocabulary and language patterns are reinforced, unfamiliar concepts discussed.
- Teacher **models** language structure by reading first 2/3 pages with students. Using **oral cloze** allows students to suggest words that fit.
- Students **read orally** while teacher **monitors reading**.

Format 2: Early Emergent, Concepts of Print, Beginning Reading Strategies

- Teacher uses **Picture Walk** to reinforce language and concepts.
- Model the reading no longer a part of the lesson.
- Students **read orally** while teacher **supports and monitors** use of **reading strategies**.
- Students **reread orally** to develop fluency.

Format 3: Upper Emergent, Reading Strategies

- Teacher covers text as students are led through **Picture Walk**.
- Teacher reinforces **reading strategies** students will use to decode words.
- Students read orally to **practice reading strategies and decoding**.

Teacher Support

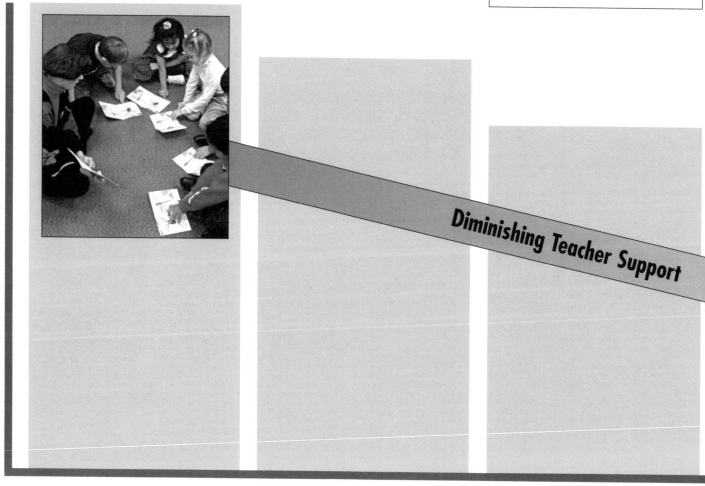

Diminishing Teacher Support

Format 1   Format 2   Format 3

During Reading: How Teacher Scaffolding Changes

The main differences in the six guided reading lesson formats occur at the During Reading stage of the lesson. This chart highlights those differences and shows how the teacher support provided through the guided reading lesson decreases as students become more proficient readers.

Format 4: Upper Emergent, Silent Guided Reading

- Students may have own copy of book.
- **Picture Walk** brief. Students encouraged to **ask own questions** about the book.
- Teacher prompts/questions **focus the reading**. Students **read silently** to find the answers.
- Students **reread book silently**.

Format 5: Early Fluency, Beginning Literature Circles

- Teacher provides prompts to **focus the reading**.
- Students **read silently** to find answers.
- Students encouraged to make own predictions.
- Students **reread** book **independently**.
- Students use **literature response journals** to record questions and comments.

Format 6: Fluency, Literature Circles

- Teacher provides book talk/summary to **focus the reading**.
- Purpose for reading established.
- Students **read** book **independently**.
- Students use **literature response journals** to record questions and comments.

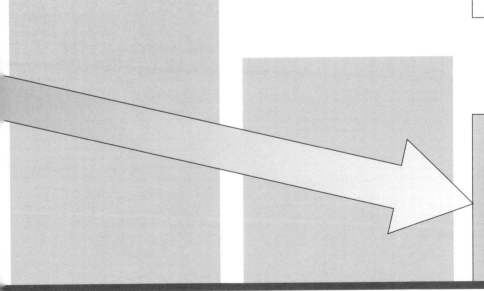

Format 4   Format 5   Format 6

The Before Reading and After Reading segments of the guided reading lesson follow a similar format. The difference lies in the sophistication of the discussion in the Build Comprehension section of the lesson. Students at early fluency and fluency levels will be able to analyze text features and literary elements in more detail than less experienced readers. These charts highlight the process that occurs Before and After Reading.

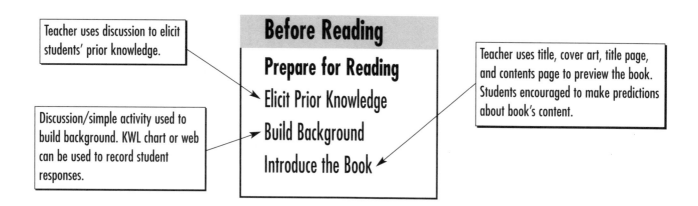

Teacher uses discussion to elicit students' prior knowledge.

Discussion/simple activity used to build background. KWL chart or web can be used to record student responses.

Before Reading

Prepare for Reading

Elicit Prior Knowledge

Build Background

Introduce the Book

Teacher uses title, cover art, title page, and contents page to preview the book. Students encouraged to make predictions about book's content.

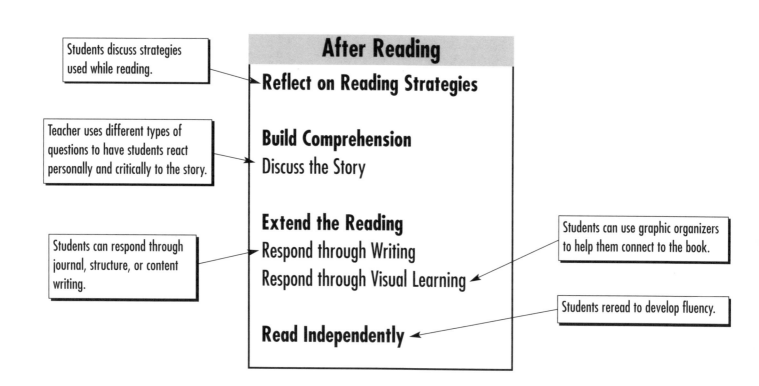

Students discuss strategies used while reading.

Teacher uses different types of questions to have students react personally and critically to the story.

Students can respond through journal, structure, or content writing.

After Reading

Reflect on Reading Strategies

Build Comprehension
Discuss the Story

Extend the Reading
Respond through Writing
Respond through Visual Learning

Read Independently

Students can use graphic organizers to help them connect to the book.

Students reread to develop fluency.

Early Emergent	Upper Emergent

Early Emergent

Focus on Schema Cues
- What do you know about _____?
- Have you ever _____?

Focus on Concepts of Print
- Where do you start reading?
- Put your finger on the first word.
- Which way do you read?
- Now where do you go to read the next part?
- Can you find the title page?
- Point to the title.

Focus on One-to-One Correspondence
- Point to each word as you read.
- Read it with your finger.
- Did that match?
- Were there enough words?

Focus on the Meaning Cues
- Did that make sense?
- What happened in the story when _____?
- Use the pictures to make sure what you read made sense.

Focus on Structure Cues
- Did that sound right?
- What might be another way to say that?
- Can you think of another word that would fit here?

Focus on Graphophonic Cues: Locating Known Words
- Can you point to _____?
- Show me _____.
- How did you know that word was _____?

Focus on Graphophonic Cues: Locating Unknown Words
- Can you find _____?
- How did you know that word was _____?
- What do you think that word might be?

Focus on Cross-Checking
- How did you know that word was _____?
- Is there another way to tell?
- It could be _____, but look at _____.

Focus on Self-Correcting
- Take a closer look at _____.
- Were you right? Could it be _____?
- How did you know that this word was _____?
- Can you find the tricky part?

Upper Emergent

Focus on Schema Cues
- What do you know about _____?
- Have you ever _____?

Focus on the Meaning Cues
- Did that make sense?
- What happened in the story when _____?
- What do you think it might be?
- Were you right?
- Use the pictures to make sure what you read made sense.

Focus on Structure Cues
- Did that sound right?
- What might be another way to say that?
- What is another word that would fit here that looks right and makes sense?

Focus on Graphophonic Cues
- Did you use what you know about sounds and letters to decode the word?
- What letter/sound does it start/end with?
- What would you see at the beginning/in the middle/at the end?
- Do you know another word that might start/end that way?
- Is there any part of the word that you already know?
- Does that look right?

Focus on Cross-Checking
- How did you know that word was _____?
- Is there another way to tell?
- It could be _____, but look at _____.

Focus on Self-Correcting
- Take a closer look at _____.
- Were you right? Could it be _____?
- How did you know that this word was _____?

Focus on Self-Monitoring
- Try that again.
- What did you see?
- Were you right?
- How did you know?
- Why did you stop?

Early Fluency	Fluency
Focus on Schema Cues • What do you know about _____? • Have you ever _____?	**Focus on Schema Cues** • What do you know about _____? • Have you ever _____?
Focus on Meaning Cues • Did that make sense? • What happened in the story when _____? • Were you right? How do you know?	**Focus on Meaning Cues** • Did that make sense? • What happened in the story when _____? • Were you right? How do you know?
Focus on Structure Cues • Did that sound right? • Is there another way to say that? • What is another word that would fit here? Why?	**Focus on Structure Cues** • Did that sound right? • Is there another way to say that? • What is another word that would fit here? Why?
Focus on Graphophonic Cues • Did you use the parts of the word that you know to figure it out? • Did you look at the whole word?	**Focus on Graphophonic Cues** • Did you use the parts of the word that you know to figure it out? • Did you look at the whole word?
Focus on Self-Correcting • You had a tricky word on this page. Which word was it? • Are you right? Could it be _____? • Take a closer look at that word and try again. • What do you know in the word that could help you?	**Focus on Self-Correcting** • You had a tricky word on this page. Which word was it? • Are you right? Could it be _____? • Take a closer look at that word and try again. • What do you know in the word that could help you?
Focus on Cross-Checking • How did you know that word was _____? • Is there another way to tell? • It could be _____, but look at _____.	**Focus on Cross-Checking** • How did you know that word was _____? • Is there another way to tell? • It could be _____, but look at _____.
Focus on Self-Monitoring • Try that again. • What did you notice? • Were you right? • How did you know? • Why did you stop?	**Focus on Self-Monitoring** • Try that again. • What did you notice? • Were you right? • How did you know? • Why did you stop?

Reading group: _Josh, Mia, Tina, Jorge_

Date	Title	Level	Challenging Concepts	Difficult Vocabulary/ Sentence Structure	Strategies	Skills	Comments	Assessments
Monday 11/18	The Tree House	B	tree house	sentence structure on last page	• point to words • initial sounds	• z • short vowel /u/ • short u • up	Josh had trouble with last page. Others doing well with one-to-one correspondence.	Mia—92% on Assessment of Reading Behavior
Tuesday 11/19	The Big Hill	B	climb	sentence structure on last page	• directionality • point to words	• r • review short u • review up	Directionality and one-to-one correspondence is coming along for all students.	Tina—93% on Assessment of Reading Behavior
Wednesday 11/20	Rat's Funny Story	B	(none)	ha-ha-ha pattern	• return sweep	• review r • on	Focus on return sweep with Mia, Josh, and Jorge.	Josh—90% on Assessment of Reading Behavior
Thursday 11/21	Mrs. Wishy-Washy's Tub	B	tub (bathtub, bath)	wishy-washy	• return sweep	• alliteration /w/ • w • short i • review short u • is, on	Group still doing well with one-to-one correspondence. Mia doesn't have return sweep yet.	Jorge—90% on Assessment of Reading Behavior
Friday 11/22	The Bridge	B	meanies	bridge number words oh-oh	• return sweep • directionality	• segmenting and blending • final x • short i • on	Return sweep used on every page. Everyone is doing better.	Concepts of Print Checklist—shows all four students are developing one-to-one correspondence and directionality

This example is based on books from *The Story Box Reading Program*

Reading group: _____

Date	Title	Level	Challenging Concepts	Difficult Vocabulary / Sentence Structure	Strategies	Skills	Comments	Assessments

Scoring:

<u>Words</u> ____ = Error Rate 1: ____   Accuracy Rate ____%   SC Rate 1: ____
Errors

Reading Level: ____ Independent ____Instructional ____ Difficult
Seen text ___   Unseen text ___

For this title: Reading Fluency

____ to ____ errors = Independent   ____ Fluent

____ to ____ errors = Instructional   ____ Word by word

____ or more errors = Difficult   ____ Not fluent

Retelling

	Complete	Adequate	Limited
Characters	____	____	____
Setting	____	____	____
Events	____	____	____

Prompted ____

Unprompted ___

Comments: _____

_____

Comprehension Check

Literal:

Inference:

Critical:

Creative:

Comments:

Skills Check

Phonological Awareness:

Phonics:

High-Frequency Word:

Other:

Comments:

Comprehension and Skills Check Score

____ Complete   ____ Adequate   ____Limited

Overall Reading Proficiency

Reading   + Comprehension   = Reading Proficiency Score
Level_____   & Skills Score _____

____ Independent   ____ Instructional   ____ Difficult

Comments: _____

_____

_____

Assessment of Reading Behavior

Name _____

Date _____

Book Title _____

Reading Level: _____ Independent _____ Instructional _____ Difficult

Level _____

Assessment of Reading Behavior

E	SC	Text	Cues Used* Errors			Cues Used* Self-Corrections			Comments
			M	S	V	M	S	V	

After the reading, have the child retell the story.

< Totals   * M = meaning,   S = structure,   V = visual

Assessment of Reading Behavior

Error and Accuracy Rates

Error Rate	Accuracy Rate	Reading Level
1:200	99.5%	
1:100	99	
1:50	98	Easy/
1:35	97	Independent
1:25	96	
1:20	95	
1:16	94	
1:14	93	
1:12.5	92	Instructional
1:11.75	91	
1:10	90	
1:9	89	
1:8	87.5	
1:7	85.5	
1:6	83	Difficult
1:5	80	
1:4	75	
1:3	66	
1:2	50	

Accuracy/Reading Level	Comprehension Level	Overall Reading Proficiency Level
95–100 (Independent)	Complete	Independent
	Adequate	Independent
	Limited	Instructional
90–94 (Instructional)	Complete	Independent
	Adequate	Instructional
	Limited	Difficult
85–89 (Difficult)	Complete	Instructional
	Adequate	Difficult
	Limited	Difficult
Less than 85 (Difficult)	Complete/Adequate/Limited	Difficult

Bibliography

Adams, M. Jager. *Beginning to Read: Thinking and Learning About Print.* Cambridge, MA: MIT Press, 1990.

Allington, R. L., and S. A. Walmsley, eds. *No Quick Fix: Rethinking Literacy Programs in America's Elementary Schools.* Newark, DE: International Reading Association; New York: Teacher's College Press, 1995.

Au, K. H, J. H. Carroll, and J. A. Scheu. *Balanced Literacy Instruction: A Teacher's Resource Book.* Norwood, MA: Chistopher-Gordon Publishers, 1997.

Brown, K. J. "What kind of text—for whom and when? Textual scaffolding for beginning readers." *The Reading Teacher* 53, no. 4 (December 1999/January 2000): 292-307.

Braunger, J., and J. P. Lewis. "Building a Knowledge Base in Reading." Portland, OR: Northwest Regional Educational Laboratory's Curriculum and Instruction Services, National Council of Teachers of English, International Reading Association, 1997.

Calfee, R. "Assessing Critical Literacy: Tools and Techniques." *In The First R: Every Child's Right to Read,* edited by M. F. Graves, P. van den Broek, and B. M. Taylor. New York: Teacher's College Press; Newark, DE: International Reading Association, 1996.

Cheyney, W. J., and E. J. Cohen. *Focus on Phonics.* Bothell, WA: Wright Group, 1999.

Christie, J., B. Enz, and C. Vukelich. *Teaching Language and Literacy: Preschool Through the Elementary Grades.* New York: Longman, 1997.

Clay, M. *The Early Detection of Reading Difficulties.* 3d ed. Exeter, NH: Heinemann, 1985.

Clay, M. *An Observation Survey: Of Early Literacy Achievement.* Portsmouth, NH: Heinemann, 1993

Cunningham, P. M. *Phonics They Use: Words for Reading and Writing.* 2d ed. New York: Harper Collins College Publishers, 1995.

Fountas, I. C., and G. S. Pinnell. *Guided Reading: Good First Teaching for All Children.* Portsmouth, NH: Heinemann, 1996.

Garner, R. "Metacognition and Self-Monitoring Strategies." In *What Research Has to Say About Reading Instruction,* edited by S. J. Samuels and A. Farstrup, 236-252. Newark, DE: International Reading Association, 1992.

Glazer, S. Mandel. *Assessment Is Instruction: Reading, Writing, Spelling and Phonics for All Learners.* Norwood, MA: Christopher-Gordon Publishers, 1998.

Goodman, Y. M. "Revaluing Readers while Readers Revalue Themselves: Retrospective Miscue Analysis." *The Reading Teacher* 49, no. 8 (May 1996): 600-609.

Graves, M. F., P. van den Broek, and B. M. Taylor, eds. *The First R: Every Child's Right to Read.* New York: Teacher's College Press; Newark, DE: International Reading Association, 1996.

Harp, B. *Handbook of Literacy Assessment and Evaluation.* Norwood, MA: Christopher-Gordon Publishers, 1996.

Herman, J., P. Aschbacher, and L. Winters. *A Practical Guide to Alternative Assessment.* Alexandria, VA: Association for Supervision and Curriculum Development, 1993.

Johnson, A., and M. Graves. "Scaffolding: A Tool for Enhancing the Reading Experiences of All Students." *Journal of the Texas State Reading Association* 3, no. 2 (Fall/Winter 1996/97): 31-37.

Marlow, L., and D. Reese. "Strategies for Using Literature with At-Risk Readers." *Reading Improvement* 29, no. 2 (Summer 1992): 130-132.

McIntyre, E., and M. Pressley. *Balanced Instruction: Strategies and Skills in Whole Language.* Norwood, MA: Christopher-Gordon Publishers, 1996.

McNeil, J. *Reading Comprehension: New Directions for Classroom Practice.* New York: Harper Collins, 1992.

Morrow, L. Mandel. *The Literacy Center: Contexts for Reading and Writing.* York, ME: Stenhouse Publishers, 1997.

Richards, J. C., and J. P. Gipe. "Activating Background Knowledge: Strategies for Beginning and Poor Readers." *The Reading Teacher* 45, no. 6 (February 1992): 474-476.

Routman, R. *Invitations: Changing as Teachers and Learners K-12.* Portsmouth, NH: Heinemann, 1991.

Schwartz, R. M. "Self-Monitoring in Beginning Reading." *The Reading Teacher* 51, no. 1 (September 1997): 40-48.

Snow, C.E., M. S. Burns, and P. Griffin, eds. *Preventing Reading Difficulties in Young Children.* Washington, DC: National Academy Press, 1998.

Spiegel, D. "Blending Whole Language and Systematic Direct Instruction." *The Reading Teacher* 46, no. 1 (September 1992): 38-44.

Spiegel, D. "A Comparison of Traditional Remedial Programs and Reading Recovery: Guidelines for Success for All Programs." *The Reading Teacher* 49, no. 2 (October 1995): 618-625.

Strickland, D. S. "What's Basic in Beginning Reading? Finding Common Ground." *Educational Leadership* 55, no. 6 (March 1998b): 6-10.

Strickland, D. S. *Teaching Phonics Today: A Primer for Educators.* Newark, Del.: International Reading Association, 1998.

Tancock, S. M. "A Literacy Lesson Framework for Children with Reading Problems." *The Reading Teacher* 48, no. 2 (October 1994): 130-140.

Tierney, R. L. "Literacy Assessment Reform: Shifting Beliefs, Principled Possibilities, and Emerging Practices." *The Reading Teacher* 51 (1998): 374-390.

Tompkins, G. E. *Literacy for the Twenty-First Century: A Balanced Approach.* Upper Saddle River, NJ: Merrill, 1997.

Vygotsky, L. S. *Mind in Society: The Development of Higher Psychological Processes.* Edited by Michael Cole et al. Cambridge, MA: Harvard University Press, 1978.

Vygotsky, L. S. "Thinking in Speech." In *The Collected Works of L. S. Vygotsky. Vol. 1, Problems of General Psychology,* edited by R. W. Rieber and A. S. Carton, 39-243. New York: Plenum Press, 1987.

West, K. R. "Noticing and Responding to Learners: Literacy Evaluation and Instruction in the Primary Grades." *The Reading Teacher* 51, (1998): 550-559.